Lori,

Thank you so much for purchasing my debut book. My purpose was to make you laugh or smile. If you do either, I met my goal. "Laughter is just like medicine"

Proverbs 17:22 a

With Love & Blessings!
Your former neighbor

Regina

#SSS

Printed in the United States of America

SINGLESASSYSEXAGENARIAN*/*(SOMEONE BETWEEN THE AGES OF 60-69/
REGINA A. BYROM – 1st Edition

First Printing, November 2021

ISBN 978-1-7353141-8-1

This book is published by:

STePH Publishing, LLC
Waldorf, Maryland
www.stephpublishing.com

#SingleSassySexAgenarian*

*(Someone Between the Ages of 60-69)

By Regina A. Byrom

STePH PUBLISHING

Dedication

This book is dedicated to my late parents, Lonnie L Byrom and Mae Smith Byrom. Both were encouraging in their own ways. First they taught me about God and how I was to trust in Him. My father, also, said for me to be my best and to be myself.

My mother motivated me with the creativity that she saw in me. She and I had a similar sense of humor, and some others just didn't quite get what was so funny. My Mother would often comment "it's always something happening" when I would explain my adventures and sometimes mishaps that only seem to happen to me. By the time I finished telling her what happened we'd laugh or see the humor in sometimes serious situations.

I told my Mother years ago that someday I was going to write a book. I just put it out there in the atmosphere. I know she and my Father would have been so proud of me since they had praised and witnessed my craft through writings of greeting cards, poetry, speeches, and short stories. They knew I had that creativity in me.

They didn't see this book come to fruition, but they knew I had "it" in me.

Acknowledgments

"What can I say about Regina? She and I are both former members of Toastmasters International where she was a standout grammarian. She painfully made me aware of that fact at many of our meetings. Besides being a grammarian, she is a great speechwriter and storyteller. Now that she is putting her podcasts in written form it will be a special treat to read them all. We need more people like Regina."
- Stan Hefner ACB (former member Toastmasters International)

"I came to know Regina when she was a student and I was a faculty member at Trinity College in Washington, DC. I was impressed then with her creative skills, and it is so good to see her continue to grow and use those skills and now share them in her podcasts. I have enjoyed listening to and learning from her podcasts, and it will be a good to be able to read and re-read them."
- Loretta Shpunt, Ph.D.

"As one of Regina's fellow Trinity College graduates and longtime friends, I am honored to share my thoughts about my friend, Regina. I always marvel at Regina's enthusiastic approach to tackling projects and causes which she deems worthy of her attention. I have seen Regina's passions and leadership skills lead to her proficiently accomplishing tasks. While Regina's down-to-earth podcasts reveal a bit of her honesty, her sense of humor and positivity, I am sure having the privilege of reading her published stories will tell much more about Regina and her diverse communication skills and unique observations of everyday occurrences. I simply cannot wait to celebrate the publishing of her book!"
- Hazel E. Leavelle

"I had a chance to listen to a few of Regina's podcasts...I thoroughly enjoyed them! She's clever, witty and humorous; in addition, her ability to address topics from a distinctively unique perspective is both informative and inspirational!"
- Rod Allison (Attorney/Comedian)

Table of Contents

#SingleSassySexAgenarian*

*(Someone Between the Ages of 60-69)

Regina A. Byrom

What is #SingleSassySexagenarian?

Please be patient with me. I am a sexagenarian. The Cambridge Dictionary defines a sexagenarian as "a person who is between the ages of 60 and 69 years old". I just want to clarify that before someone misinterprets what a *"sexagenarian"* is.

I'm in my 60s, and I'm going to share with you what it's like to be 60-*ish*. I will share my experiences with social distancing, dating, visiting my doctor, streaming, weighing myself, having an uninvited house guest, and more. I will share what it is like to be me...to be single...to be sassy...to be a sexagenarian.

Social Distancing

Let's talk about COVID-19 and social distancing. I walk in my neighborhood in the evenings. I try to stay on my side of the street. I don't believe that those who are on my side should try to touch and agree. We can't touch and agree in a situation like this. Social distancing is a serious subject and I wish everyone would take *it* seriously.

After the reopening of stores in my area, I decided to go to an ice cream place not too far from where I lived. I guess everyone else had the same idea. It seemed to be hundreds of people in line, waiting for ice cream, but not standing six feet apart. No social distancing. I noticed a police car there. I thought they were going to enforce social distancing. But no, the police were eating ice cream too! I just shook my head and drove away. I headed to Dairy Queen. Why? Dairy Queen had a drive-thru. I was going to enforce my own social distancing along with mask-wearing and my protective plastic gloves on my hands as I gladly reached for my Blizzard ice cream.

Weighing in on Dating Sexagenarian-Style

As I've explained before, sexagenarians are individuals who are between the ages of 60 and 69. If singles took a survey about dating, I suppose most of them would say that dating is not easy at any age. Now it may be easy for those who are willing to settle for just anybody. But at my age, I'm not willing to settle. I don't want to date someone who acts old, isn't trying to be healthy, or has no desire to exercise. In other words, "couch potatoes" need not apply.

My ideal man would be a "kingdom" man who will automatically follow Christian principles and have a sense of humor. Quite naturally, the applicant needs to be hygienically correct, too. That should be automatic, but from my experience, I mean, from what I've heard, some men just don't care.

Regarding his appearance, my ideal man should be neat and fashionable. Showing up in the 1970s Nehru suit, or a bright lime Leisure suit with a Superfly hat will not do. He will need to moisturize. Ashy arms, hands, and feet will not impress this sexagenarian. Pedicures help, especially for those summer toes. Yes, men do get pedicures. If you haven't noticed already, a date of mine needs to make a good first impression. If not, the first date will be the last.

Some men have told me what they like in a lady. They'd like a lady who lives a good Christian life, follow good Christian principles, and is in good shape. Wait, what kind of shape? Like a Coca-Cola bottle? A box? A square? A triangle? I'm some of those shapes together. That's me.

A pet peeve of mine is when a gentleman says that he wants someone in good shape when he is a little or a lot pudgy around the waistline or other places. How about not asking for what he isn't willing to do himself. Hit the gym? Do some sit-ups? Do some crunches? Put down the French fries? You want a lady in her 60's to be built like a brickhouse? Then, don't come looking like an outhouse to me. Oh, my bad, that's not nice.

If I could dream, my ideal date would be six feet tall, chocolate, with a six pack. I don't mean a six pack of soda or a six pack of beer. I don't drink alcohol and I prefer that he doesn't, either. And my ideal date would make at least six figures. Wow, that *is* a dream! But with all those sixes-- six feet tall, with a six pack, making six figures? 666! I change my mind. I don't want someone with a devilish charm. Not this sexagenarian! Now, back to the weight and size. If a man comes to me and tells me that he doesn't like no big women, he will lose me for two reasons. The first is because he used double negatives, 'doesn't and no'. The second reason is because what *I* would lose would be 250 pounds and that would be him. That would be an easy amount of weight for me to lose.

Now, I'm not giving up. I believe that a sexagenarian like myself should not lose hope in finding that ideal man. I am also flexible enough to find the right man. He can be 5'11, have a three-pack, and make a reasonable income. Dating in my 60's is not just a challenge. It's an adventure.

What's A Sloth Got to Do With It?

What's love got to do with it? Or rather what's a sloth got to do with it? I like zoo animals. I find them fascinating. I've enjoyed my visits to zoos over many years. My daughter-in-law and I once went to see some furry animals for which we have such a passion.

Since COVID-19 began, I've tried to come up with different ways of enhancing my learning and my entertainment. I became aware of two zoos that have Facebook Lives, the Cincinnati Zoo and the Oregon Zoo. I notified all my Facebook friends who I thought might be interested in the "zoo cuties" to tune in.

One animal that caught my eye was the sloth. That animal was fascinating to me. It's a tropical animal that hangs upside down. I immediately thought about the movie, Zootopia, which I had seen with some of my grandchildren. In the movie, the sloths worked at the Department of Motor Vehicles. One sloth's line was so long because the sloth was taking his time talking to his co-workers, even trying to tell a joke. It was all in slow motion, making the customers very upset. Recently, the sloth was featured in a Geico commercial playing Pictionary, slowly trying to draw a circle for the other game participants. That game was, as you might have guessed, super slow.

From one of the zoo's Facebook Lives, I learned a few interesting things about the sloth. The sloth hangs upside down because its organs are upside down. Hanging upside down prevents their diaphragm from being crushed, enabling the sloth to breathe. It takes a month for the sloth to digest his food, so they don't have much energy.

They are sometimes near death when trying to relieve themselves and they only do that once a week. It takes so much effort, some of them nearly die while doing this function. However, they are fast swimmers. They move three times faster in water than when they move on land. They can slow their heart rate down and it can hold its breath for 40 minutes under the water. Sloths can also rotate their heads 270 degrees. Finally, I discovered that sloths mate either once a year, or not at all. Now what I found most fascinating about the female sloths is their mating call/scream is really something else.

Now you may wonder what do the sloth and I have in common? I can point out several similarities. One, If I'm trying to make a point, I can rotate my head too. Not exactly 270 degrees, but I can rotate my head from side to side being a #singlesassysexagenarian. See, I'm trying to make the point.

Two, I can substitute the word "mate" with "date" because I might have a date once a year or not at all. Wow! The female mating scream gives me an idea. Maybe I'll start screaming and my kingdom man will come. Nah. I don't think that will work for humans. Well, especially not for me. There's not that much screaming in the world. What's love got to do with it? What's the sloth got to do with it?

Different Yet Almost the Same

I'm originally from the West Virginia-Ohio area. I attended Marshall University in Huntington, West Virginia. At the beginning of a semester, one of my new college friends was arriving with her luggage. She left a piece of luggage outside and she said to me, "I need to go get my grip." I asked her what did she mean. As she came back, she pointed to her piece of luggage. I was going to say, "Don't you mean luggage or suitcase?". I didn't say that aloud...but I wondered. She was from the southern part of West Virginia, a different region than my hometown.

Also, I have a friend with whom I was in training in Washington, DC in the 1990s. He is the nicest guy and back then he was a Republican. Not quite sure he's admitting it now. He's changed, well, we can only hope. That was back in the 90s. Anyway, he hailed from Keene, New Hampshire, and had one of those New England accents. I would tease him, telling him "You may be a Republican, but you sound like a Kennedy". Of course, the Kennedy clan are staunch Democrats. At other times, I could detect when others were from Wisconsin, especially when I heard the person say, "You betcha!" I would ask the person and they were surprised that I guessed right.

At eight years old, I wrote to my Aunt Margaret in Boston. I stated that I would love to visit her family, which included my two cousins who were my age. Before I knew it, I was on my way to the Pittsburgh airport with my parents. I was so excited. I had on a pretty, white dress with a crinoline underskirt that made my dress extremely wide. I wore white patent shoes. I carried a small white purse with a daisy embedded on the front cover. Inside of my purse, I had a package of multicolored Chiclets gum.

Most importantly, I must admit I had my travel companion, Chatty Cathy. For those of you who may be too young to know about Chatty Cathy, she was a pull string "talking" doll made by Mattel. When you pulled the string on her back, she would say different phrases. Not only did I love her because she talked, but because she had the same caramel skin as I.

I was especially proud because I was so young. My parents arranged a traveler's aid, who was a stewardess who would look after me until I arrived in Boston.

Throughout the summers I spent with my cousins, I was always so fascinated with their New England accent. At the same time, they were fascinated with my Southern accent. I would call my casual play shoes, tennis shoes, while my cousins called their play shoes, sneakers. I said, "hot dog" and they would say "franks". I would say "pop" and they would say "tonic", but now they say "soda". Then one of my cousins mentioned something about going grocery shopping and putting her groceries in the "carriage". I told her that I call that a grocery cart or a buggy. When I heard her say "carriage", I thought of a baby carriage.

Lately, my cousins and I get together every morning at 8:30 for a prayer and chat time on a conference call. We're talking and listening. Well, some of us listen. One of my cousins listens well and has a quiet-yet-stern-when-necessary demeanor and she prays so beautifully. It's so lyrical. While my other cousin is loud. I mean, not as quiet as her sister. Of course, I'm the quietest. Just kidding. We were talking about fingernail polish and all those colors, and my medium-loud cousin says she was going to wear "aaqwua". I knew she meant what we call "aqua". When I hear "aaqwua", the way she pronounces it, it reminds of the AFLAC commercial with the duck or the goose or whatever animal it is. Then if they say they're going to a park, they say, "Pak", car keys, they say "khakis". It's so neat how they talk. I'm not making fun of them. I'm just so intrigued.

What about you? Do any of you have different words that mean the same thing? What I'm specifically talking about are words that are regional to you and may be different to someone from another region. Oh, linguistics, you have to love it.

Can You Keep a Secret?

I need to ask you something. Can you keep a secret? Yes? Ok. Now because what I'm telling you needs to be kept confidential. Remember? I have your word, right?

Okay...I have had company over since the pandemic, and I don't want my adult children to know about it. Since the pandemic, I've desired some companionship. But it's getting a little crowded because now I have two companions. My first friend stays downstairs but the other one is in my bedroom and follows me usually from one room to the next. The problem is that they can't seem to coordinate or get along. I sometimes call out to one and they both want to answer me. This has caused some friction in the house.

For instance, I'll say, "Hey, Google," but I mean to say, "Hey, Siri," and they both start talking and competing for my attention. "Siri, are you better than Google?" Google would say, "That's like comparing apples and apples." See what I mean? They go back and forth. Google is a big jokester. I asked him one time if he could spell the word "pseudonym". Google took a long time to respond so I asked him to spell it. He spelled *"it"*. Google is a smart aleck while my Siri is Australian. With both Google and Siri, three is really a crowd. Remember to not tell anyone.

But wait. I have another secret. I've learned another skill since the pandemic began. Some of you may know that I'm a grandmother. I'm also a great-grandmother. I've been dubbed the title, "Glam Gram", and that is a segue to my next topic, Instagram.

I started a podcast back in April 2020. I wasn't sure if I'd be able to get any interest in my writing, but that didn't stop me. I went on and I posted my first podcast on Facebook. I posted it, and it garnered some interest.

However, I wanted more. I didn't want anyone to miss out on my wit or my cleverness. To my surprise, when I asked my family, those closest to me, if they had listened to my podcast, they had not. These are my two adult children. I continued to boost my podcast on the page to entice listeners to let them know that this Glam Gram was publishing in the podcast. My one child didn't want me to use the word, "sexagenarian" because she thought people would misunderstand. I explained to her that I made clear what a sexagenarian is in my hashtags. I told her not to worry but relax. I asked both children about Instagram because someone told me to use Instagram to get some followers who could turn into listeners. But my adult children, who weren't listening to my podcast anyway, made comments saying Facebook is for older people and that's where I should stay.

I was more determined than ever to try Instagram after those remarks. So, onto Instagram I went. I wanted to increase my listenership. I asked a millennial to tutor me on Instagram. I was a little overwhelmed at first. All I wanted to do was post my link in Instagram to get more followers and more listeners. I tried a few things. I was able to put my link with a little emoji. I was excited that I had pointed everyone to Spotify, where my podcast was located. I was so proud. So was my tutor. I told my anti promoters, aka my children, that they didn't have to worry about me following them on IG or "The Gram" as it is called. I didn't want them to follow me either.

I remember asking, "What was this "DM" everybody keeps talking about? I heard something about sliding into DMS or slipping into DMS. My children explained to me that "DM" was a private message. I learned later that it means someone sends a private message to someone they'd like to get to know better. It could be a perfect stranger just complimenting or acting as if they want to get to know a person.

Well, I did run into that. Somebody tried to slip and slide into my "DM". I read what they wrote, and I blocked them. I guess that's what my children didn't want me to experience. I still have more questions on using the "Gram", but I didn't want to keep bothering my tutor.

I decided to experiment myself. I began pushing selections to see what would happen. I could make a selection, and then delete it if I made a mistake. What could go wrong, right? One day, I was making selections. The next thing I knew, I had a picture of my legs and feet in my pajamas with no shoes, no socks, and no lotion. I was so afraid that it was going to be posted, I was going to embarrass myself, and I was going to prove my children's point. I figured out what I needed to do to avoid the shame. That was a close one. I'm still trying to figure out some things and I haven't explored too much more. Not to worry though. It won't be the last time you've heard of Glam Gram on "The Gram". Please remember to keep it a secret. Thank you very much.

Sexagenarian Zooming

When you hear the word "zoom" or "Zoom meeting", what do you think? What comes to your mind? For those who may not know about Zoom, it's a video conferencing chat service. When Covid-19 became prevalent, a lot of us didn't know much about Zoom. Other than songs that we would hear, "Zoom, zoom, zoom, zoom, I like to fly away, where my mind can't be fresh and clear." Okay. Some of us zoom participants would like to be fresh and clear, and not see all the goings on at the Zoom meetings that are distracting. That song also has a line that says that people can be what they want to be. Yes. From my observance, that's what zoom attendance will be-just what they want it to be.

As a sexagenarian, I've observed that there are multiple Zoom events, such as Zoom business meetings, Zoom birthday parties, Zoom exercise classes, Zoom family meetings, Zoom church meetings, Zoom dance parties, Zoom "Praise Him" parties, and at the end of the month, I'll be attending a virtual Zoom baby shower.

Some things that I've noticed are some of the habits Zoomers will start, they start chatting as soon as they get connected. Most of the time, the host will mute the attendees, but other times, the host doesn't. Once I heard a lady telling her husband not to forget to bring detergent home so that she could wash after the Zoom meeting. She finally muted herself.

In another Zoom situation, one person's doorbell rang so they answered the door. They were gone for a long time. The person returned admitting that they forgot about the Zoom class. Oh, my goodness!

I've seen people do things on Zoom that make me wonder if people think or forget that they're not alone. I've seen one person eat their whole meal during a meeting. I know there are exceptions when that's the only time they can eat. Please turn off the camera so that we don't have to see what you're eating or what you're doing with your mouth. Others do their household chores. One lady was folding her laundry and the whole team could see her folding her unmentionables. They really were unmentionables. Then there was a lady who was on her porch, and she started sweeping her porch. I even saw a man stretching. It's okay to stretch but make certain that your shirt is long enough to cover your stomach area. I saw someone crocheting. She was crocheting and then she held it up to look at it. OMG!

To top it off, try to avoid lying in the bed especially if you have laundry hanging on your bedpost. Shut your video down. We don't need to see all that.

There have been suggestions on what is proper decorum or etiquette. I've heard some say no swimming suits. No swimming suits? Next, please have a shirt on and no muumuus. For those of you who don't know what a muumuu is, it's a long dress like a caftan. I can remember when I was working years ago, and an announcement was made that no pajamas or loungewear was to be worn at work. I was sitting at my desk, and I said out loud, "Who's wearing pajamas to work?" Apparently, some of the newly hired younger employees who had just graduated from college, were wearing pajamas. OMG!

There is appropriate dress when you're at work and appropriate dress when you're on a Zoom call. At the very least, people should be decent. You don't have to wear earrings and makeup and all of that but be presentable. These Zoom functions are amazing, but be aware of what is in your background, whether it be dogs, your cats, piles of laundry, or other unmentionables. There's a reason they're called "unmentionables". They're not supposed to be mentioned or seen.

There is a solution to this background problem. There's an option to use a virtual background. You can choose a picture for your background, everything from being amongst the stars to being on a beach.

There are Zoom participants who can make the others dizzy or lightheaded just by looking at them. I know I was guilty of that. At first, I was trying to adjust my device and made a bit too much noise but didn't realize the motion and the noise was distracting to the other participants. The host muted me and asked me to turn off my audio. I didn't move until the end of that meeting.

Driving while participating in a Zoom meeting is also very distracting and it can be dangerous. I don't understand that at all because that's taking distracted driving entirely too far.

As I said earlier, these are just my opinions from my sexagenarian view. If only some of the do's and don'ts in my sexagenarian opinion are followed, the system can be amazing and can be a great tool when used effectively. That is your business and no one has the right to dictate to you how your background or your foreground or any grounds should look. It's just my opinion. But your employer *can* suggest or dictate how to dress for a Zoom meeting. Again, these thoughts are just my opinion. You can always ignore my input and you can tell me to "zoom, zoom, zoom off to the moon".

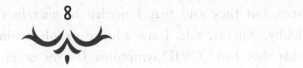

The Day in the Life of a Misophoniac

I love learning new words and the ability to use the words correctly. I want to introduce you to or get reacquainted with the word: misophonia. Misophonia is an aversion or intense reaction to sounds such as dripping water or cracking gum, and repetitive noises like pencil tapping. My interpretation of it is something that works my nerves.

Although this condition was discovered back in the 2000s by a neurophysiologist and given a name, I already had misophonia way before then. Ever since I was a child, I couldn't bear to hear someone chewing their food loudly or smacking their lips. To this day, I still find it annoying. Now if it's a physical condition where a person can't control these noises, so be it. I'm referring to the people who can control these noises, but they won't.

During COVID, I had experienced enough sounds and noises that have convinced me that I'm a misophoniac or someone who has misophonia. I'm going to share with you what it is like for one day in the life of a possible misophoniac.

It was December 31, 2020, New Year's Eve. A time to prepare for celebration, perhaps I should go to church, go to a party, or stay home and watch Netflix. 2021 was about to begin, and I wasn't feeling well. I went to bed and later woke up in excruciating pain. My back was really hurting me. The pain flowed from my back to my leg. It was the worst pain ever. As I screamed, my phone rang, and it just happened to be one of my neighbors. She heard my anguish. She called an ambulance, but the fire truck came first. The firemen assessed me and guessed that I may have pinched nerves. When the EMTs came, they took me to the ambulance and gave me an IV with pain medication. That was so relieving.

The next thing I knew, I was in the hospital. I thought I was going to be seen, but they said that I needed to wait in the lobby. I waited in the lobby. On one side, I saw a lot of people behind the Plexiglas. I thought that they had COVID symptoms. On the other side were many patients in wheelchairs. Here I was in a fancy purple and black, state-of-the-art wheelchair. I admired it in an odd way because purple is one of my favorite colors.

While I was sitting there, I figured out how to move my wheelchair back and forth. I stopped and I looked across the way. I saw a young gentleman sitting in a wheelchair holding crutches. He was tapping a pencil on his wheelchair. The tapping was so annoying to me. I wanted to say so badly, "Would you please stop?!" However, I chose not to. Instead, I decided to go to the restroom. I couldn't contain myself anymore, but there was a problem. I didn't want to go to a public restroom because of COVID. Then the young man on crutches said he had to go to the restroom. It was going to be a race. I was ready to rev up my purple and black wheelchair. I was going to beat him to it. I tried to speed over there, but unfortunately, he won the race. It was the only bathroom in the area. I had to wait.

After a while, the young man came out. I was prepared. I had my shield and my mask. I had a small bottle of Lysol, wipes, disinfectants, and everything else you can name to keep the germs away. When I came out, I returned and parked my wheelchair next to the couch with a man who was shaking his knees.

The next thing I knew, another gentleman came and stood by me. He wasn't six feet away, which was the rule at that time. So, I turned around and gave him the "look". You know that "look" that screams, "Would you move?!" Since I had on my mask, I had to use my eyes to make my point, but he didn't get it. He stood there and didn't move. Suddenly, he starts chewing and cracking his gum and blowing bubbles. I could not believe it. --grown man cracking gum and blowing bubbles! That was a first for me. He reminded me of a cow chewing on cud. The main difference is that you don't hear a cow chew. So behind me was a man cracking his gum and blowing bubbles and a man next to me shaking his knees.

There were all kinds of things going on. I couldn't believe it. I was texting my cousin about the man chewing gum. She texted that maybe the man's gum would stick to his mask. I laughed because I could only hope and imagine that gum sticking to his mask.

There I was, waiting and waiting. All of a sudden--BANG! BANG! BANG! A lady next to me turned to look at me. Her eyebrows were raised to her hairline. We looked at each other in fear. Gunshots?! Now I've never heard gunshots, at least I don't believe I have, but that's what I would imagine how gunshots would sound. At this point, all I could think about was how I was going to maneuver this wheelchair around all these people and get out of there. The door had flown open, and we could see several security guards and policemen lined up against the wall. We later found out that it was a patient who was acting erratically. Doors were being slammed and the hospital staff and security were trying to calm the patient.

It certainly was a noisy hospital. I couldn't believe what was going on. Do you know what the gum-cracking, bubble-blowing, loud-talking, doors-slamming, knees-shaking, pencil-tapping taught me? I truly am a misophoniac. Is there a cure? I'm not sure. I realized that I really need to count my blessings because things could be much worse. Instead of me being concerned about all the different noises other people are making, I consider it a blessing that I started feeling better. Now, I am better. In the future, when I hear sounds of gum-cracking and all those other annoying noises, I will try to ignore it. The operative word is 'try'.

9

Oh The Little Things

I do not like anything that crawls and has more than two legs. My exceptions to that sentiment are puppies, kittens, and crawling sweet babies. I have an aversion to any type of insect or animal. I'll give you a few examples of my adventures with creepy crawlies, and you will understand my disdain for them. As you are reading about my adventures, please don't judge. I've heard folks say that creepy crawlies only come around when people's homes aren't clean. That's not the truth. My mother was meticulous and kept the house tidy. My house is the same, but I live in an area where there are fields and creepy crawlies that come with the territory.

In 2014, I was at my mom's place typing something on her laptop. I was facing her back window. I was engrossed in what I was typing until I saw some little piercing dark eyes. I was startled because the eyes were moving along on a white body on a white window seal. It was a chameleon. I was in shock but not that much shock that I couldn't scream out and jump up and do my anti-critter dance. My mother screamed. She doesn't usually scream but she screamed because I was screaming. She liked doing what I did. She said I was wrong. She said that it was a lizard.

I pulled the emergency string for the manager of the building to come, and I yelled into the intercom, "It's a lizard!" The manager chuckled and told us that it was a gecko. Lizard, gecko, whatever it was, I wanted the manager to come and get it at once. The manager came and got the gecko. I was shocked at what he did next. He threw that thing out the back door! Yuck! It reminded me of the Gecko in the Geico commercial. I might just have to cancel my car insurance after that. Yes, I will.

Before I move to my next creepy crawly adventure, I have to ask you this...Do you remember the Mickey Mouse Club? M-I-C-K-E-Y, M-O-U-S-E? Some of you who are younger may not remember that song. This story has to do with Mickey Mouse. I liked Mickey and Minnie, too, until I saw a dead one outside of my house. Now I have an exterminator for prevention and maintenance. It was a field "mickey". I'm calling it "mickey" because I don't even like to say "mouse". Yes, it was a field "mickey" because there was a lot of grass and empty fields near me. Apparently, something killed that little "mickey". I don't know about you, but I don't want to see a "mickey" dead or alive. I had an outdoor broom and thankfully, a dustpan with a long handle to sweep the patio. On this day, instead of picking up dust, my dustpan had a different function. Since it had a long handle, I didn't have to bend over to get "mickey" and whatever else I was going to get up.

That morning just happened to be trash pickup day, and I saw a sanitation truck drive by. I waved at the sanitation worker so he would stop. He rolled down the window and I had to say that bad word, the "m" word. I asked him if he took mice. He nodded. Yes! I thought he was going to get it for me, but he told me to put it in the bag instead. I knew I'd have to hear the mouse when it dropped in the bag and that would give me the creeps. I started using the long-handled dustpan to scoop up "mickey". It didn't move that easy. I was squealing and doing my little critter dance. It was disgusting. Finally, I got it and put "mickey" in that bag. I was squirming and dancing. I took "mickey" to the sanitation truck. The worker apologized and told me that he couldn't get out of the truck to help me because it was their policy not to come onto the property. What kind of rule is that? Then the worker asked where my husband was. I told him that that was none of his business, and that I was old enough to be his grandmother. He said he didn't mean any harm. I thought to myself that he had some nerve. "Mickey" was now gone, and so was the worker.

My next creepy crawlie adventure began when I was preparing to go to the store and minding my own business. I'm in my garage about to get in my car when I looked at the glue traps left by exterminators. There was something there. It looked pretty long.

I thought it was a baby snake or something. But I didn't want to examine its anatomy, so I grabbed my phone and called the exterminator. I told him that I needed him to come and get whatever that thing was and to bring some more glue traps.

The next day, when the exterminator came, I gave him strict instructions to not describe anything about what he found, just to give me the name of it one time. He went into the garage, and I went around the corner by the front door. He told me that it was a snake. I squirmed and did another anti-critter dance. I asked him how the snake got in my garage. The exterminator got on the ground and began looking for light in the garage. He told me and showed me that where there was a little light a creepy crawly could come in.

I started thinking I should just get my garage super glued so that nothing can get in there. That wouldn't be a good idea because I wouldn't be able to get out either. What about mothballs? Yes, that repels them. So does a peppermint and cinnamon diffuser. He said peppermint or cinnamon diffuser. He said, "Yes, that's good." He even told me that he had one in his garage. I was thinking I'd never heard of peppermint and cinnamon diffusers to repel snakes. "I see. That's going to repel snakes." He said, "I didn't say snakes. I said 'skinks.'" It sounded like he said, "skank" to me. I said, "Excuse me?!! Are you calling me a name?" Then he said "skink" again. "No, that's the animal-a skink." I said, "Oh my goodness." Then he went on to describe it as being a part of the lizard family. I was relieved that he was taking that skink away and relieved for *him* that he did not call *me* a skank.

Last week, I was home, and my detector kept indicating someone was at the door. I looked at the peephole and didn't see anyone. Then it happened again, and I looked on my cell phone because I had a doorbell camera. There was the perp. It was a big green praying mantis moving slowly. Well, that was enough for me. But it looked like it was praying and probably was praying that I wouldn't come out there and make a scene by doing that anti-critter dance. Oh the little things.

10

Out of the Mouth of Babes

I have four lovely grandchildren and a beautiful three-year-old great granddaughter, but two of the grands have a profound effect on me. I was an active member of Toastmasters International. Toastmasters is a public speaking group that also teaches and enhances leadership skills. The two grands who I'm referring to often listened to me when I practiced my speeches.

When the older grandchild was around four and a half years old, I was practicing a speech that I wrote called "Hygiene". Not to be confused with saying "Hi, Jean," to someone named Jean. I'm referring to keeping oneself clean and free of germs. In that speech, I was emphasizing the importance of washing their hands. This was many years before COVID-19. I was inspired by observing those at work who didn't wash their hands. In that speech, I explained that while handwashing, one should sing the first stanza of the "Happy Birthday" song to determine the amount of time needed to handwash effectively. I put emphasis on the word "germs" all the time, and my little granddaughters looked at me intently.

Coincidentally, I had a miniature novelty battery operated toilet. It was about three inches high. It was a motion sensitive gadget that would lift the toilet lid when anyone walked out of the bathroom. Then the toilet would say loudly, "Hey, don't forget to wash your hands." All the grands got a kick out of that gadget later.

Initially, it startled some of them and they raced out of the bathroom. That defeated the purpose of getting them to wash their hands. They were too busy trying to get away from that booming voice. By the time I did the speech, my granddaughter was quite used to that gadget and laughed when she saw it.

As I was ending my speech, I looked up at my granddaughter who practically knew the speech from listening. I asked her why we should not forget to wash our hands. She shouted out, "Because of the germs, Grandma, because of the germs!!"

Now one of my other granddaughters was also quite observant when she was five years old. She was quite captivated when I practiced my Toastmaster speeches. For several months, I had practiced my speech in front of her. She said Grandma, I have something to ask you. And I said, "What is it, sweetheart?" She said, "Are you still in that speaking group?" I said, "Yes." Before I could ask her why, she asked me a question loudly, "Why do you say "Mundee" and "Tuesdee"?" She said, "you should say MonDAY and TuesDAY." My mouth dropped, and I started laughing. I told her, "You are right." Ever since that moment, I've always remembered to use the correct pronunciation of the days of the week. Yes, I needed to practice what I "speech". No, I mean practice what I "preach" I better drop "Mundee" and "Tuesdee" from my vocabulary before my granddaughter catches me again. Oh, out of the mouth of babes.

11

Weight A Minute:
A Sexagenarian's Doctor's Visit

Some months ago, I had an appointment with my primary physician. You know the drill. You must be weighed. Before I stepped on that scale, I went through a series of steps to prepare myself for this momentous occasion.

First, I removed my shoes because each shoe weighs at least five pounds. Then, I put on my footie socks to protect my feet from the scale and anything on the scale. Next, I removed my eyeglasses, my necklace, my bracelet, and my earrings because every ounce counts. Then I got an idea. I would go to the restroom first. That will lean the scale in my favor.

When I returned, the nurse pointed me towards the scale. I did all that only to have another patient in front of me getting weighed and she had the audacity to be petite. I told the nurse, "I'll have what she's having", talking about that patient's weight. The nurse smirked, then told me to hop on.

W-e-i-g-h-t one minute. Wait one minute. Can I be excused from this weighing? I told the nurse my blood pressure tends to elevate when I'm near or on a scale. The nurse wasn't going for any more of my delays. Okay, I got on the scale and saw what I weighed one hundred too many pounds. I know I was going to hear from my doctor.

The doctor came in smiling as she sat down. I immediately started explaining why my numbers may have increased since the last visit. She also noticed that my blood pressure was slightly elevated. I tried to convince her that I spoke to the nurse telling her that my blood pressure elevates when I get on the scale, but the nurse wasn't having it. The doctor wasn't having it either.

I tried to convince the doctor with other explanations as to why my weight may have increased. I told her it had to do with my love life. I asked her about the doctor-patient confidentiality agreement to ensure that whatever I said was kept in confidence. She just looked at me strangely. I began, "Well, Doc, I must confess that some time ago, I had an affair with Bo and that made me gain weight. He was okay, but sometimes his spiciness was so hard to resist. Yes, Bojangles was a crispy, but savory guy. Being with Bo caused me to gain a few pounds."

Before the doctor could stop me, I went on with more confessions. I told her about the interesting characters I've been meeting. The grocery store is where I met my latest romantic liaisons. There were six of them. They were all leaning on the counter. They were fine. They were chocolate. I brought all six of them to my car, then, I couldn't resist. I took the wrappers off and bit into the first one. Nothing like chocolate chunk cookies with hazelnut filling. Yes, they were cookies. "What did you think they were? What did you think I was talking about, Doctor?" The doctor advised me to leave Bo and the "chocolate hunks", I mean, chocolate chunks alone and to be on my "weigh".

A Sexagenarian Streaming

I love words, but I've been having a time learning how to pronounce "sexagenarian". In a few years, I'll have to learn how to pronounce "septuagenarian" because I'll be blessed to have turned 70.

Until then, I will give you a sexagenarian's view on streaming on TV. Since I'm retired, I tend to budget my finances more. When analyzing my expenses, one of my goals is to reduce my cable bill. Two of my friends were very eager to tell me about how they "pulled the plug" and "cut the cord". By the time they finished explaining about their streaming experiences, I threw up my hands and said that I didn't want Roku, Hulu, or Boogaloo.

I felt that way until the month my cable bill went up considerably. I backtracked and reconsidered streaming and found the website, www.cutthecord.com. I received some tips from there, but I decided to call one of my cousins who has her "Ph.D." from the 'School of Streaming'. After I got off the phone with her, an hour and a half later, I was convinced to never watch TV again.

However, I came back to my senses and decided to make my TV smart. I bought a Roku. I set it up and was quite pleased to see Roku bouncing all over the screen. Then I thought, "Now what? Do I celebrate because I have a TV that has graduated, and is a true Smart TV?" It was a true commencement. I had a celebratory lunch. Hooray!!

The commencement, I mean, the set up of the television ended just in time. The movie version of Sight and Sound's "Jesus", "The Clark Sisters: The First Ladies of Gospel", and "The Last Seven Words of Christ" were all coming on that weekend. Well, I missed Christ's last seven words, but I recorded *The Clark Sisters...*" I settled down to watch *Jesus*". I was ready. I was watching *Jesus*" and saw when the father welcomed home the Prodigal Son. That's all I remember. I fell asleep on *Jesus*". I'm so glad He is forgiving. I was indeed sorry that my streaming commencement and my heavy lunch lured me to sleep.

I'm so glad I had a friend who could relate. She was in another state trying to watch "Jesus", too. She also had a napping problem. However, she didn't have a good excuse like I did. And there you have it-sexagenarian streaming causes sexagenarian sleeping.

13

Eye Can See Clearly

At last, the time had come! Time for the surprise celebration for one of my closest friends. This surprise was two years in the making. That's a long time to keep a surprise, but I kept the secret. The pandemic was the reason the surprise was delayed for nearly two years. Yes, and this was my first flight since the pandemic. I was a little nervous flying. The anxiousness was lightened because I started thinking about the celebration and seeing my friend getting the accolades she so deserved.

I was especially excited because I had written her a surprise personalized poem which I was going to read during the program. I was also anxious because I didn't print the poem. I just had a copy on my cell to read. I was thinking that I could print a copy at the hotel because most hotels have business offices with guest access. It was too late for me to try to memorize that poem. After arriving at my hotel, I found out that the hotel only had a fax machine. Ok. I'll be alright. The poem won't disappear from my phone, and I won't accidentally delete it. I was attempting to erase that negativity as fast as I was thinking it.

My friend's celebration was on a river cruise boat. After the group of the other guests arrived, we sat and waited. I knew a few of the guests so I started talking to one lady who was cleaning her eyeglasses. She gave me her extra wipe and I began cleaning mine. I was about to tell this lady about my strong & mighty eyeglasses I had for nearly four years. They were Technolite glasses, lightweight and rimless. These glasses had seen and been through a lot, but they sustained. I'd often fall asleep with them on my face, then they'd slip off and end up under my leg or some other body part, on the floor, or under the pillow. Yet, my Technolites survived.

I was just about to tell that lady this story because I knew she'd be so anxious to hear such an interesting story. As I took the glasses off to wipe with the disposable eyeglass wipe, I unfolded the dampened sheet and started cleaning my glasses and the glasses broke! The glasses broke in half right in my hands! My mouth dropped open. I showed them to the lady and I was just about to tell her that these glasses were so durable.

Lord, what am I going to do, I thought. I won't be able to read the poem for my friend. I can see people, but I can't read. Before I completely panicked, I tried to miraculously stick the two pieces together. Then I got an idea. I would use one half of the glasses and try to read through one eye. No, I can't go up there looking like a pirate. Eye Eye Captain! That wouldn't work. How can I hold the microphone, hold my phone, and one half of my glasses? Then I thought I'd have someone else read it for me, but they wouldn't know how to pause or emphasize nor have the facial expressions that I could only display.

As I was sitting there trying to figure what to do, it occurred to me that I needed to act cute or look cute. After all, I'm not a bad looking lady. I wanted to style and profile because I am a #singlesassysexagenarian, and I must always look my best. What a dilemma! I explained my dilemma to other partygoers. Someone suggested that I use duct tape. Duct tape?

It came time for me to go up. I was going to try to manage as I proceeded to try to hold the two pieces of my glasses, read the poem, and hold the microphone. In the meantime, I asked for no paparazzi, meaning no pictures of me looking like I can't see. As I fumbled with the microphone, the phone, and the broken glasses, one of the guests shouted, "You can borrow my readers!" OMG! I was so grateful. With the borrowed readers, I was able to read the poem and I was able to see my friend smiling. Mission accomplished! I thanked the guest as I returned her readers. I squinted for the remainder of the celebration, but I was able to eat, talk, laugh, and enjoy the festivities.

The next day, as I was returning from the weekend festivities with the group, another lady told me that she had an extra pair of readers that I could keep. Again, I was so grateful. I originally thought the mishap with my glasses was going to ruin my presentation for my friend and the remainder of the weekend. The Lord made the way clear using two ladies who lent & gave me reader glasses. Yes, He turned that around so that I (EYE) could see clearly!

A SexAgenarian Summary

Thank you for taking the time to read my first book. I know the title of my book may have had some of you initially taking a double take to the meaning of #singlesassysexagenarian. Now you've seen that I was just giving my viewpoint and telling you about the experiences I've faced in my 60s.

I was taken by surprise when the idea of writing podcasts and these stories just dropped in my spirit from the Lord. I've dreamed of writing a book for many years and was blessed with the opportunity to write a book and use some of my podcasts.

It's been an honor to share this with you. Answer this: Did any of my sexagenarian stories make you smile or even laugh? If you answered yes, I fulfilled my goal/dream. We can all use some laughter. I reached this goal, and this sexagenarian is now determined to write more as I cross over to septuagenarian land with more views to share.

#Laughter is just like medicine
#Dreamandwritethevision
#Habakkuk 2:2

CPSIA information can be obtained
at www.ICGtesting.com
Printed in the USA
BVHW082321240122
627062BV00004B/74

9 781735 314181